THE PEACE OF CHRISTMAS

THE
PEACE
OF
Christmas

QUIET
REFLECTIONS
FROM
Pope
Francis

Diane M. Houdek

franciscan
media
Cincinnati, Ohio

Cover and book design by Mark Sullivan
Cover image © iStock | Liliboas

LIBRARY OF CONGRESS CONTROL NUMBER:
2017949546

ISBN 978-1-63253-171-1

Published by Franciscan Media
28 W. Liberty St.
Cincinnati, OH 45202
www.FranciscanMedia.org

Printed in the United States of America.
Printed on acid-free paper.
17 18 19 20 21   5 4 3 2 1

For Rob, Becky, Evan, and Ashlyn:
being part of your holiday activities
has brought a special grace to my life

Contents

INTRODUCTION: THE TWELVE (OR FORTY) DAYS
OF CHRISTMAS ... *xi*

THE GIFT OF GRATITUDE ... *1*

THE GOD OF SURPRISES ... *4*

MAKING A LIST AND CHECKING IT TWICE ... *7*

BALANCING EXPECTATIONS ... *10*

CHRISTMAS IS FOR CHILDREN ... *13*

CREATOR OF THE STARS OF NIGHT ... *16*

EMMANUEL—GOD WITH US ... *19*

THE WOMAN AT THE HEART OF THE CHRISTMAS STORY ... *22*

WHAT DO OUR DECORATIONS SAY? ... *26*

IT STARTED WITH ST. FRANCIS ... *29*

KEEPING CHRISTMAS SIMPLE ... *32*

GENERATIONS OF ORNAMENTS ... *35*

The Crib and the Cross ... *38*

Knowing We Have Enough ... *41*

Overcoming Our Doubts and Insecurities ... *44*

The Paradox of the Incarnation ... *47*

When You Eat and Drink, Remember Me ... *50*

Learning Generosity ... *53*

Reaching Out in Mercy ... *56*

"He Kept Christmas in His Heart" ... *59*

Letting Ourselves Be Loved ... *62*

Those Long-Standing Traditions ... *65*

Let There Be Light ... *68*

The Empty Chair ... *71*

Light in the Darkness ... *74*

The Power of Love ... *78*

Seeing with the Eyes of God ... *81*

The Challenge of Christmas ... *84*

THE WHOLE WORLD BEING AT PEACE ... *87*

THE WONDER OF AN INFANT ... *90*

A TIME FOR FAMILY ... *93*

WHEN OUR FAMILIES DON'T SEEM SO HOLY ... *96*

MARY, MOTHER OF GOD ... *99*

AS THE YEAR DRAWS TO A CLOSE ... *102*

A FLIGHT INTO EGYPT ... *105*

FOLLOW THE STAR ... *108*

ARISE, SHINE, GO FORTH ... *111*

OUR LIFE IS A JOURNEY ... *115*

RETURNING TO NAZARETH ... *118*

SOURCES ... *121*

Introduction

THE TWELVE (OR FORTY) DAYS OF CHRISTMAS

*W*hen is the Christmas season? Different groups will give different answers. Retailers, of course, would have us believe it begins as soon as the Halloween candy is whisked off the shelves. Religious tradition says that it begins on December 25 (with a vigil or eve the night before) and lasts through January 6, the source of the iconic Twelve Days of Christmas. In the liturgical calendar it lasts another week, ending on the Feast of Baptism of the Lord.

For most people, the reality falls somewhere in between. The long Thanksgiving weekend is often when they begin to put up decorations. Festive light displays at local parks and shopping districts begin around the last week in November. Neighborhoods glow with multicolored lights and decorations that range from tasteful to garish.

For all the stories of out-of-control shopping binges and fist-fights in the aisles of Walmart over the season's hottest toys, most of us have found ways to balance the many sides of Christmas in our homes and families.

The in-between season of Advent offers us a chance to experience some calm before the holiday storm. I love Advent. For most of my adult life I've lived alone, so it's easy for me to settle into the silence, the darkness, the candlelight, contemplative Advent music, the readings from the prophets of longing and anticipation. My time is my own, and I can choose what activities to participate in. But it's somewhat churlish and inhospitable to say no to every Christmas party simply because the Church calendar says it's still Advent. And I do enjoy decorating the house. Sometimes I begin early in December; other times I wait until shortly before Christmas Eve.

I grew up with a gradual movement toward Christmas through the month of December. A box of Christmas picture books came out of storage around Thanksgiving. We prayed around the Advent wreath as a family, but the Feast of St. Nicholas on December 6 was a tiny foretaste of Christmas. Mom set up the Nativity set on the dining room buffet and, if I was good, I could add straw to the empty manger so Jesus would have a soft bed. The spruce tree mysteriously appeared on the porch in mid-December but wasn't decorated until one night a few days before Christmas. The week between Christmas and New Year's Day was spent visiting family and friends.

Even the most faithful users of Advent devotionals can find themselves forgetting the readings for Christmas and the days after as routines change with the holiday break. The wonder of the Christmas event itself can get lost in the celebration. *The Peace of Christmas* offers an opportunity to reflect with Pope Francis on the many moods and challenges of one of the central realities of our faith: Our God became one of us, came to dwell in our midst, and began life as we all do, as a tiny baby, needy and vulnerable and dependent on the people around him for his very survival.

Pope Francis knows that Christmas is many things to many people, often changing with the times and circumstances. Our experiences—good and bad—in the months since last Christmas will color our emotions and even alter our activities during the holidays. God chose to become one of us, letting his human life be shaped by the time and place in which he was born. In the same way our lives are shaped by the world around us. But because of the incarnation, the changes are wrapped in an awareness of eternity, of something beyond us and greater than us, but still intimately part of us. In the midst of all the stress and busyness of the season, this truth reminds us that the true gift of Christmas is something money can't buy.

If you follow the reflections from beginning to end, you'll notice a pattern from Thanksgiving through December and Christmas to the beginning of the new year and the celebration of Epiphany. But while the book is divided into daily reflections, it's designed more for browsing than marching through day by day. Keep it someplace handy and pick it up when you have (or need!) a few minutes of quiet. Turn to its pages when you feel frustrated with the hectic pace of preparations or when you feel suddenly struck by the wonder and beauty of this season. Let the words of Pope Francis move you to a new appreciation of the incarnation. Let his quiet reflections offer some balance and perspective to the world around you and the swirl of emotions within you.

Each reflection has a brief quote from Pope Francis, followed by a bit of a reality check on what's happening in our lives during this season. Sometimes the two complement one another. Sometimes the contrast between the ideal and the real might encourage us to make some changes in our thoughts and the actions that flow from them. Each reflection closes with a "gift" to enhance your experience of the season. It might be a gift you give to another, it might be a gift you receive, it might be a gift of something intangible, like time or hope or a glimpse of what lies beyond this world. It's a small daily reminder that all of life is gift and that the Christmas season celebrates our greatest gift from God.

The Gift of Gratitude

Saying "thank you" is such an easy thing, and yet so hard! How often do we say "thank you" to one another in our families? These are essential words for our life in common. "Sorry," "excuse me," "thank you." If families can say these three things, they will be fine. "Sorry," "excuse me," "thank you." How often do we say "thank you" to those who help us, those close to us, those at our side throughout life? All too often we take everything for granted! This happens with God too. It is easy to approach the Lord to ask for something, but to go and thank him: "Well, I don't need to." I think of the ten lepers in the Gospel who were healed by Jesus. They approach him and, keeping their distance, they call out: "Jesus, Master, have mercy on us!" (Luke 17:13). They are sick, they need love and strength, and they are looking for someone to heal them. Jesus responds by freeing them from their disease. Strikingly, however, only one of them comes back, praising God and thanking him in a loud voice. Jesus notes this: ten asked to be healed and only one returned to praise God in a loud voice and to acknowledge that he is our strength. Knowing how to give thanks, to give praise for everything that the Lord has done for us.

A Christmas Reality

Thanksgiving in America began with noble sentiments and is surrounded by traditions, rituals, and stories of hardship, sharing, and giving thanks for survival in a new land. A friend of mine, widely known for her cooking skills, often bemoaned the fact that her children, even as adults, wouldn't let her vary the turkey and trimmings menu. I'm amused when grocery stores helpfully group all the ingredients for a Thanksgiving meal in the center aisles for convenience and as a help to those who cook only occasionally and have no idea what they need.

We might think that the commercialization of Christmas is a twenty-first century phenomenon, but the classic 1947 movie *Miracle on 34th Street* reminds us that the Macy's Thanksgiving Day parade has long been the kick-off to the retail Christmas season. In just the last decade, we've seen the creep from crack-of-dawn Black Friday shopping sprees to late-night Thanksgiving deals, to all-day Internet shopping on Thursday. Each year there's a growing movement to discourage stores from being open on Thanksgiving Day on the premise that it's not fair to the people who have to be away from their families due to work schedules. And it's OK to have one or two days a year with no shopping.

But we need to remember that gratitude is at the center of this day of giving thanks. It's not a bad way to begin the hubbub of the Christmas season. Gratitude helps to keep our expectations reasonably in check. It reminds us that what we have can always somehow be enough.

Your Christmas Gift Today

Begin (or continue) a gratitude journal. It can be as elaborate as a beautiful blank book or as simple as a sticky note on your desk or the kitchen counter. Write it by hand or type it into a notes app on your phone. But find something to be thankful for every day. And don't just think about it in passing. Take the time to record it, honoring the importance of gratitude in your life.

The God of Surprises

The Word of God is living. And therefore it comes and says what it wants to say, not what I expect it to say or what I hope it will say or what I want it to say. The Word of God is free and it comes as a surprise, since our God is the God of surprises: He comes and always does new things. He is newness. The Gospel is newness. Revelation is newness. Anyone who is a man or a woman of hope—the great hope which faith gives us—knows that even in the midst of difficulties God acts and he surprises us.… God always surprises us.… But he asks us to let ourselves be surprised by his love, to accept his surprises. God surprises us. It is precisely in poverty, in weakness, and in humility that he reveals himself and grants us his love, which saves us, heals us, and gives us strength. He asks us only to obey his word and to trust in him.

A Christmas Reality

Some people love surprises; some people hate surprises. I suspect that it has something to do with how much we trust, whether it's other people, the universe, or God. If our experience has been that of having our needs and desires met with some consistency, we can trust that the future will continue to be positive. If we've known abuse or disaster or a complete lack of control over what happens to us, we may see surprise as something to be avoided at all costs. We will plan and predict and do all we can to see around the next corner.

We've all known (or perhaps been) people who ferret out the secret stash of Christmas gifts in the weeks leading up to the holiday, even unwrapping and rewrapping a package to see what's in it. We want to know rather than being surprised. While I never went that far, I often had a general sense of what I might get for Christmas. We were big on lists in our family. But one year my dad built me a mountain dulcimer from a mail-order kit because my mom told him I had been looking at one. I was completely taken by surprise on Christmas day at the unexpectedness as much as the skill and care he had taken in the building of it.

Pope Francis reminds us that from the moment of creation, God has been surprising us with new things, unexpected things, things that we could never have imagined. Through the eons and centuries, God has surprised his people with all that they needed to survive and thrive: food and water in the desert, descendants as numerous as the stars in the heavens, new lands and renewed hope, forgiveness and mercy and love beyond telling.

YOUR CHRISTMAS GIFT TODAY

We get glimpses of God's surprises every day if we're paying attention. Let yourself be surprised today by the beauty of nature's changing seasons, by the generosity and kindness of friends and strangers.

Making a List and Checking It Twice

*F*irst of all, I would like, with you, to thank the Lord for all his gifts. For it is true that in these days one thinks of Christmas presents, but in reality the one who gives the true gift is he, our Father, who gives us Jesus. Our presents, this beautiful tradition of exchanging presents, should express precisely this: a reflection of the unique gift that is his Son made man and born of the Virgin Mary.

A Christmas Reality

The tradition of Santa Claus developed in many cultures from the actions of the fourth-century St. Nicholas, a bishop who helped many poor people with gifts to rescue them from destitution. Like all the saints, this holy figure lived the Gospel and followed the example of Jesus, giving freely to others and showering gifts on them in imitation of a gracious God.

Over the centuries, we've confused Santa and God, or perhaps we've created both in an image that was never intended to be theirs. Both are portrayed as keeping a careful account of each good and bad thing we do, weighing our actions against a standard of perfection, recording a black mark each time we make a mistake. It may be a reflection of a strongly authoritarian culture, or it might just be a parent's desperate attempt to keep antsy kids from misbehaving in the excitement and anticipation of the Christmas season: "Santa's elves are watching you!"

Pope Francis reminds us that God's attitude toward us is far more one of mercy than of judgment. Forgiveness and generosity are the hallmarks of the divine. The psalms tell us that God puts behind himself all our sins. Gifts, by their nature, are something we don't deserve and can't earn. And the greatest gift-giver is our God. If this is what our faith tells us, then our Christmas traditions should reflect this.

YOUR CHRISTMAS GIFT TODAY

We don't always realize how many of the things we learn as children stay with us into adulthood and color our perspectives. If you have a tradition of Santa Claus or Father Christmas in your family, take a lovingly critical look at how it plays out with your children and grandchildren through the season. Try to resist the temptation to use Santa as a threat against misbehavior and instead encourage them to imitate Santa's generosity. Take a few minutes to recall the way Santa was presented when you were a child. Keep the good traits and gently let go of the negatives.

Balancing Expectations

A Quiet Reflection from Pope Francis

*I*n a few days, we will have the joy of celebrating the birth of the Lord: the event of God who became man in order to save us; the manifestation of the love of God who does not just give us something, or send us a message or a few messengers, but gives us himself; the mystery of God who took upon himself our humanity and our sins in order to reveal his divine life, his immense grace and his freely given forgiveness. It is our encounter with God who is born in the poverty of the stable of Bethlehem in order to teach us the power of humility. For Christmas is also the feast of the light which is not received by the "chosen," but by the poor and simple who awaited the salvation of the Lord.

A Christmas Reality

I suspect that even when we made Christmas lists by paging through the Sears and J.C. Penney catalogs, we chose things that were ridiculous, extravagant, beyond our families' means, or just not right for us. I desperately wanted a Lite-Brite set and an Easy-Bake Oven. I'm fascinated that I still remember it all these years later, but not getting them didn't ruin my life. And I also remember the things I did get: a basketball, a bike, collectible Steiff animals, stacks and stacks of books, and even the socks and underwear that Grandma always got us. The toys and games kids want today are fancier and more expensive, but the same principles still apply. What we want, what we expect, and what we get won't always match. At the same time, we might be surprised by something far beyond what we ever could have imagined.

Somewhere in the course of a childhood or a lifetime, we learn to balance expectations and reality. It has much to do with learning the difference between wants and needs. We rarely do this perfectly in our everyday lives. It's even more difficult in the heightened atmosphere of Christmas, whether it's visions of sugar plums dancing in our heads or the bells and whistles of this year's electronics. Sometimes what we imagine as the perfect Christmas present fails to live up to its hype, and we're disappointed. Sometimes something that seems mundane and utilitarian proves to be valuable in ways that go far beyond the glitz and sparkle of Christmas morning.

Pope Francis reminds us that those who know how truly needy they are may be closer to understanding God's gifts and receiving them with the proper spirit of grateful acceptance. If we think we already have everything we need and focus only on wanting something bigger and better, we may let disappointment overwhelm us and blind us to God's immense goodness.

Your Christmas Gift Today

Recall one of your favorite Christmas gifts, whether it was decades ago or as recent as last year. Take some time to think about what made it special. Then think about something you wanted and didn't get. How much difference did that make in your life? How can these memories shape your expectations for this Christmas? How might they shape your reaction to the many gifts of God every day of the year?

Christmas Is for Children

*A*s we see, we know little of the Child Jesus, but we can learn much about him if we look to the lives of children. It is a beautiful habit that parents and grandparents have, that of watching what the children do. We discover, first of all, that children want our attention. They have to be at the center—why? Because they are proud? No! Because they need to feel protected. It is important that we too place Jesus at the center of our life and know, even if it may seem paradoxical, that it is our responsibility to protect him. He wants to be in our embrace, he wants to be tended to and to be able to fix his gaze on ours. Additionally, we must make the Child Jesus smile in order to show him our love and our joy that he is in our midst. His smile is a sign of the love that gives us the assurance of being loved. Children, lastly, love to play. Playing with children, however, means abandoning our logic in order to enter theirs. If we want to have fun, it is necessary to understand what they like, and not to be selfish and make them do the things that we like. It is a lesson for us. Before Jesus we are called to abandon our pretense of autonomy—and this is the crux of the matter: our pretense of autonomy—in order to instead accept the true form of liberty, which consists in knowing and serving whom we have before us. He, the Child, is the Son of God who comes to save us. He has come among us to show us the face of the Father abounding in love and mercy.

A Christmas Reality

Often we hear the phrase "Christmas is for children" and while it may seem like a cliché, it really is true. Children have an ability to abandon themselves to the joy, the anticipation, the expectations of this marvelous holiday that we lose when we become adults with responsibilities and budgets and hard economic realities. They enter into preparations with a glee that knows nothing of the perfect Pinterest project or decorations inspired by glossy magazines.

I love the insight Pope Francis reveals when he talks about "abandoning our logic to enter theirs." Watching children create worlds out of their imaginations and doing our best to take part in their visions shows a respect for God's movement within them and reminds us of our own more carefree days. There's no doubt that the pope follows the one who encouraged us to become like little children: dependent, needy, but open to the grace and protection and providence of God.

YOUR CHRISTMAS GIFT TODAY

Find ways to include children in your Christmas preparations as well as the celebration of the day itself. Let them decorate their rooms themselves. Encourage them to help with decorating cookies, even if they use half a bottle of colored sugar on one cookie in the beginning. Overlook the five ornaments on one branch of the tree because that's where the four-year-old could reach. Take delight in the Fisher-Price donkey on the roof of the stable where an adult would put the star. Christmas reminds us that there's more to life than the workaday adult world.

Creator of the Stars of Night

The Christmas tree placed beside the Nativity scene comes from the Scurelle Forest, at the foot of the Lagorai mountain range, surrounded by beautiful nature, with flowers, plants and crystal-clear streams that run along its trails. The beauty of that scenery is an invitation to contemplate the Creator and to respect nature, the work of his hands. We are all called to draw near to creation with reflective wonder. The tree and the Nativity scene thus form a message of hope and love, and help to create a Christmas spirit that can draw us closer to living with faith in the mystery of the birth of the Redeemer, who came to this earth humble and meek. Let us be drawn to the manger in a childlike spirit, because it is there that one understands God's goodness and one can contemplate his mercy, which was made flesh in order to soften our gaze.

A CHRISTMAS REALITY

One of my favorite Advent hymns gives this reflection its title. There's something wonderful about including the cosmos in our Christmas celebrations. I grew up with fresh-cut Christmas trees, usually a short-needled double balsam. It would appear on the enclosed front porch one day, lying on the swing in the cold Wisconsin air for a week or so before it came in the house. There was always something magical about bringing this little piece of the forest in the house. The artificial trees that have become more practical in my adult life never quite match that splendor.

Christmas can become a celebration of artifice and manufactured wonders. From the dangling icicle lights along the roofline to the inflatable cartoon characters on suburban lawns, we run the risk of treating this holiday as a time of one-upping not only the neighbors but also God. But we know deep down that no factory in China can produce something as wonderful as the tiniest miracle in God's creation.

Each year, the pope blesses a Christmas tree and crèche in St. Peter's Square at the Vatican. As we see in this reflection from Pope Francis, there's a protocol of recognizing with gratitude the origin of the tree and the people whose gift it is. It serves as a reminder of the many connections among us, but also the connection with nature that has been a part of the human race from the beginning of creation. Redemption is about more than a perfection of human behavior. Scripture tells us that all creation is redeemed in the coming of the Christ. It's good to remind ourselves of that as we decorate our homes and yards for the season.

Your Christmas Gift Today

As you plan your holiday decorations, find a way to incorporate something natural in the mix. It might be a real pine or boxwood wreath on the door, a freshly cut Christmas tree, a Christmas cactus, a dish of paperwhite narcissi, or a showy amaryllis bulb. Not only do these remind us of God's natural world, in many cases we can watch the miracle of life as they grow and bloom throughout the season.

Emmanuel—God with Us

he grace of God has appeared, bringing salvation to all" (Titus 2:11). The words of the Apostle Paul reveal the mystery of this holy night: The grace of God has appeared, his free gift. In the Child given to us, the love of God is made visible. It is a night of glory, that glory proclaimed by the angels in Bethlehem and by ourselves as well, all over the world. It is a night of joy, because henceforth and forever, the infinite and eternal God is God with us. He is not far off. We need not search for him in the heavens or in mystical notions. He is close at hand. He became man and he will never withdraw from our humanity, which he has made his own. It is a night of light. The light prophesied by Isaiah (see 9:1), which was to shine on those who walked in a land of darkness, has appeared and enveloped the shepherds of Bethlehem (see Luke 2:9).

A Christmas Reality

The Advent name for God is Emmanuel. We sing it over and over in the familiar hymn, "O come, O come, Emmanuel." The name means "God is with us" and comes to us from the prophet Isaiah. Matthew's Gospel reminds us that Jesus was a fulfillment of this prophecy, God with us in the flesh, born a human baby, like us in all things. It's an echo of the more exalted language of the prologue of John's Gospel, which tells us that the Word was made flesh and dwelt among us. Scripture scholars tell us that the second half of John's Greek phrase translates literally as "pitched his tent among us." This was an image that a first-century, semi-nomadic people would understand.

In the Old Testament, God's presence among the people was often described as a messenger or angel of the Lord. But the revelation of the incarnation is that now it is God himself in our midst and one of us. It's difficult for us to grasp this concept. Perhaps this is why Matthew and Luke make such a point of describing the baby in the manger visited by shepherds, the child receiving gifts from the magi. Perhaps this is why we have such a resonance with Christmas. We understand the great gift of life in a newborn child. There's a purity in a newborn, a sense of both innocence and ancient wisdom, that gives us a glimpse of God.

Knowing that God not only knows but experienced what it was to be a human being, composed of blood and flesh and bone, limited by all the things that limit us, should give us patience with our weakness and joy in our strength. In our prayers for help, we can say, "You know what it's like," and be confident that he does. But we can also look to the end of the story and know that by being one of us, he was able to raise us up to overcome those limits—and the final limit of death itself. As St. Irenaeus put it so well, "He became human so that we might become divine."

YOUR CHRISTMAS GIFT TODAY

The holiday season with its hustle and bustle and seemingly endless activities places demands on our bodies as well as our spirits. We can, if we like, imagine Jesus in the busy days of his preaching and teaching and healing ministry. If we do, we may also hear him calling to us and saying, "Come aside and rest for a while." Because we know that he knows what it is to feel tired and need to be rested and refreshed.

The Woman at the Heart of the Christmas Story

A QUIET REFLECTION FROM POPE FRANCIS

At the message of the angel, she does not hide her surprise. It is the astonishment of realizing that God, to become man, had chosen her, a simple maid of Nazareth. Not someone who lived in a palace amid power and riches, or one who had done extraordinary things, but simply someone who was open to God and put her trust in him, even without understanding everything: "Here I am, the servant of the Lord; let it be with me according to your word" (Luke 1:38). That was her answer.

God constantly surprises us, he bursts our categories, he wreaks havoc with our plans. And he tells us: Trust me, do not be afraid, let yourself be surprised, leave yourself behind and follow me! Today let us all ask ourselves whether we are afraid of what God might ask, or of what he does ask. Do I let myself be surprised by God, as Mary was, or do I remain caught up in my own safety zone: in forms of material, intellectual, or ideological security, taking refuge in my own projects and plans? Do I truly let God into my life? How do I answer him?

Take Mary. After the Annunciation, her first act is one of charity towards her elderly kinswoman Elizabeth. Her first words are: "My soul magnifies the Lord," in other words, a song of praise and thanksgiving to God not only for what he did for her, but for what he had done throughout the history of salvation. Everything is his gift. If we can realize that everything is God's gift, how happy will our hearts be! Everything is his gift. He is our strength!

A CHRISTMAS REALITY

If there's ever a time for to-do lists, December is that time! We have so many things that we need to keep straight. Shopping and parties, children's school plays and recitals, decorating, cooking, baking, and more shopping. We have work projects that need to be finished before everyone takes off for a Christmas break. We receive endless reminders for end-of-the-tax-year donation opportunities. In churches, too, all of this activity is mirrored in retreats and religious education activities and the many liturgies and prayer services of the season.

In the midst of all this rushing around and checking off items, we can forget why we're doing what we're doing. And we can miss God calling us to do something else—not one more item on the to-do list, but something radically different. It might be as simple (and complicated!) as taking an entire Saturday to play with the children instead of rushing to four different activities. It might be reevaluating what we've planned to spend on gifts and making a donation to charity instead. It might be looking at our work and hearing God suggesting that something else might be closer to what he wants us to do.

Again today, Pope Francis reminds us that God is fond of surprising his people in big and small ways. And he shows us Mary as an example of someone so open to those surprises that she became the very Mother of God. Mary is at the heart of the Christmas celebration, a model of both action and contemplation. When God became flesh, became one of us, he took on that flesh through this young woman with a spirit open to surprise and wonder and possibility.

Your Christmas Gift Today

Take a look at your to-do list for today. Select one item that you can cross off in order to spend an hour with God. Be as creative as you like in how you spend that time. But make sure the focus is on being present to God and open to the ways he might want to surprise you.

What Do Our Decorations Say?

The crèche and Christmas tree are symbols of Christmas always evocative and dear to our Christian families: They recall the Mystery of the Incarnation, the Only Begotten Son of God made man to save us, and the light that Jesus brought to the world with his birth. But the crib and the tree touch the hearts of all people, even those who do not believe, because they speak of brotherhood, intimacy, and friendship, calling all men and women of our time to rediscover the beauty of simplicity, of sharing, and of solidarity. They are an invitation to unity, harmony, and peace; an invitation to give space, in your personal and social life, to God, who does not come in arrogance to impose his power, but offers us his omnipotent love through the fragile figure of a Child. The crib and the tree, therefore, bring a message of light, of hope, and of love.

A Christmas Reality

The three things that are always part of my holiday decorations are the Advent wreath, the Nativity scene, and the Christmas tree. These might be simple or elaborate, depending on my mood and time and energy limitations from year to year, but they always appear in some form. The candles on the Advent wreath may not get lit every night, but I like the possibility near at hand. The figures in the Nativity scene might be limited to Jesus, Mary, Joseph, and perhaps a sheep, or they might include a throng of villagers about their daily work and stopping to worship the Christ child. The tree might have only lights, or it might have a collection of ornaments stretching back to my childhood.

Trees and Nativity scenes are often part of public Christmas displays as well, sometimes with not a little controversy. I enjoy seeing them blended with holiday symbols of other faiths as well. We can learn so much from one another if we're open to it. I like what Pope Francis says here about the message of unity, harmony, and peace. We know when religious symbols are being used as messages of arrogance and superiority. This goes against the message Jesus came to teach us, that "message of light, of hope, and of love."

Christmas is a good time to let our symbols and decorations offer a quiet witness to what we believe. Religion imposed on others is not likely to take root and grow true. But a seed planted in the heart can often surprise us when we least expect it.

Your Christmas Gift Today

Look for an opportunity to visit a collection of Nativity scenes from different cultures. If there's no place nearby to do this, make a virtual visit online. It's fascinating to see how the details vary, from skin tone and clothing to the animals in the stable. Reflect on the universal nature of our faith community and the strength we have through unity in diversity.

It Started with St. Francis

A Quiet Reflection from Pope Francis

These were also the intentions of St Francis when he invented the Nativity scene. Franciscan sources tell us that he wanted "to memorialize that Child who was born in Bethlehem," to enable "in some way that the disadvantages encountered by a newborn baby in his lack of basic necessities could be physically visible to the eyes." In that scene, in fact, "simplicity is honored, poverty is exalted, humility is lauded." Therefore, I invite you to pause before the Nativity scene, because the tenderness of God speaks to us there. There we contemplate divine mercy, which became human flesh and is able to soften our gaze.

Above all, however, he longs to stir our hearts.

A Christmas Reality

It's traditional for the pope to participate in a special tree-lighting in Greccio that recalls the origins of the crèche or *praecepio*.

Nativity sets (crèches) are a familiar part of our Christmas decorations. From family heirloom sets that have been passed down through generations to lighted plastic lawn displays, depictions of the Holy Family in the stable at Bethlehem remind us that this holiday centers on the birth of a baby.

The details have their roots in the Christmas stories in the Gospels. Luke tells us of shepherds and their flocks. Matthew tells us that exotic visitors from the east visited the young family. Matthew also reaches back to the prophet Isaiah with a reference to a donkey and an ox. But the Nativity tableau as we know it today began with St. Francis of Assisi in the Italian village of Greccio. St. Bonaventure, one of his early biographers, describe the scene in vivid detail. He wanted to see (and help the villagers see) what it really meant that Jesus was born as a vulnerable infant:

> Three years before he died, St. Francis decided to celebrate the memory of the birth of the Child Jesus at Greccio, with the greatest possible solemnity. He asked and obtained the permission of the pope for the ceremony, so that he could not be accused of being an innovator, and then he

had a crib prepared, with hay and an ox and an ass. The friars were all invited and the people came in crowds. The forest reechoed with their voices and the night was lit up with a multitude of bright lights, while the beautiful music of God's praises added to the solemnity. The saint stood before the crib and his heart overflowed with tender compassion; he was bathed in tears but overcome with joy. The Mass was sung there and Francis, who was a deacon, sang the Gospel. Then he preached to the people about the birth of the poor King, whom he called the Babe of Bethlehem in his tender love. A knight called John from Greccio, a pious and truthful man who had abandoned his profession in the world for love of Christ and was a great friend of St. Francis, claimed that he saw a beautiful child asleep in the crib, and that St. Francis took it in his arms and seemed to wake it up.

Your Christmas Gift Today

Today might be a good day to set up your Nativity scene. As you do so, recall the great gift St. Francis gave us in establishing a tradition of showing the Holy Family in a simple, very human setting.

Keeping Christmas Simple

*T*he Nativity scene also tells us that he never imposes himself with force. Remember this well, you children and young people: The Lord never imposes himself with force. To save us, he did not change history by performing an elaborate miracle. He came instead with total simplicity, humility and meekness. God does not like grandiose revolutions of history's powerful, and he does not use a magic wand to change situations. Instead, he makes himself small, he becomes a child, so as to attract us with love, to touch our hearts with his humble goodness; to unsettle, with his poverty, those who scramble to accumulate the false treasures of this world.

A CHRISTMAS REALITY

Music is very much a part of our Christmas customs and celebrations. I often play Advent and Christmas carols around the house and in the car to keep myself in the right frame of mind through the season. The hymn "People Look East" is catchy enough to get stuck in my head, especially when I'm thinking about starting my decorating. Its reference to decorating "as you are able" is something to keep in mind when we're busy decking out our homes for the holidays.

People sometimes have expectations that are way out of line with their personal circumstances, whether financial, health, emotional or something else. I've seen this in my own family, where age or illness has created a deep frustration with not being able to do everything one was once able to do. My mom finally learned to let her grandchildren do most of the decorations; now my sister is learning the same lesson after having surgery between Thanksgiving and Christmas two years in a row.

For a few years, I worked in retail at Christmastime. The only day we were closed was Christmas Day. I had no energy or enthusiasm for decorating after selling ornaments and gifts and wrapping paper for days on end. Mostly I just wanted to sleep. So that's what I did. I went to Midnight Mass and spent Christmas Day just relaxing.

The year my mom died, I also found decorating for Christmas difficult. So many memories came flooding in of Christmases past and a physical presence that was now lost. I managed to decorate a small tree, but then I couldn't bear to take it down at the end of the season. So I left it up—until the following Christmas. It felt right somehow.

If anything marks the Christmas season in the words of Pope Francis, it's simplicity, smallness, and humility. He rejoices in the gifts of lights and Christmas trees, carols and crèches, and the happy faces of children who gather to be blessed. Joy is always part of his Christmas message. But it's a joy that comes from the heart rather than from the external trappings that we sometimes mistake for essentials.

Your Christmas Gift Today

Think honestly about your circumstances this year. Don't be afraid to cut back on some of the cooking and baking, the decorating, the parties, if that seems like a right and healthy thing to do. Jesus doesn't need a fancy party for his birthday and neither do we. Love and peace, wholeness and health, are worth more than any decorations.

Generations of Ornaments

I would also like to thank the little "artists" who decorated the tree, and I congratulate them: You are still very young, but you have already displayed your work in St. Peter's Square! This is wonderful. Have courage, continue! This is how Michelangelo started out! The ornaments depict your dreams. These aspirations which you carry in your hearts are now in the most fitting place, because they are near the Child of Bethlehem: They are entrusted to him, who came to "dwell among us" (see John 1:14). Indeed, Jesus did not simply appear on the earth, he did not dedicate a little of his time to us, but rather he came to share our life and to embrace our aspirations. Because he wanted, and still wants, to live here, together with us and for us. Our world, which at Christmas became his world, is close to his heart. The Nativity scene reminds us of this: God, in his great mercy, came down to us to remain with us forever.

A Christmas Reality

I have very few ornaments on my tree that don't have some kind of sentimental meaning or significance, even if it's only a memory of where and when I acquired them. Some were gifts from dear friends. Many were handmade by my mom and grandma. I have a section on the tree with memories of my home state, even though I haven't lived there for over thirty years. While hanging them on the tree, I recall hobbies and enthusiasms, toys from childhood, hopes for the future. They represent music and nature, pets and wild animals, travels across the country and around the world. They remind me of where and how I've lived.

I don't hang all my ornaments every year. A few always make an appearance. Others are remnants from years when I had a bigger Christmas tree. I love telling the stories of them to people who visit. They become a way to connect past, present, and future, in much the same way that religious art functions in expressing and sharing the stories of our faith.

Your Christmas Gift Today

Look for a special ornament this year. It doesn't need to be expensive. It doesn't need to be fancy. It just needs to hold a thought, a memory, a dream of who you want to be in God's eyes. Each year when you hang that ornament on your tree, you can say a little prayer for that intention.

The Crib and the Cross

*T*here is a straight line between the manger and the cross where Jesus will become bread that is broken. It is the straight line of love that gives and saves, the love that brings light to our lives and peace to our hearts. That night, the shepherds understood this. They were among the marginalized of those times. Yet no one is marginalized in the sight of God, and that Christmas, they themselves were the guests. People who felt sure of themselves, self-sufficient, were at home with their possessions. It was the shepherds who "set out with haste" (see Luke 2:16).

A Christmas Reality

The parish where I grew up had an elaborate Nativity scene set up at one of the side alcoves each year. It was handmade by one of the parishioners, and above the traditional stable was a replica of the sanctuary of our parish church. It was a lovely way of pulling together the events of the birth of Jesus with the Eucharist that we celebrated each Sunday at Mass, and the impact of the visual connection was more immediate than any explanation could have been.

Many years ago now, the great Scripture scholar Raymond Brown put out a condensed version of his work on the infancy narrative called *An Adult Christ at Christmas*. Some people thought he was being critical of Christmas traditions and celebrations. In reality, he was reminding people that there's more to our faith than a cute baby in the manger. The incarnation and the passion, death, and resurrection are all part of the saving gift of God. Jesus didn't stay a little baby. The manger was eventually empty, and he moved into his calling as an adult. He outgrew his swaddling clothes as he would later throw off the wrappings of death.

We think of the shepherds as quaint figures in our Nativity scenes, an excuse to have all those cute sheep and lambs gamboling about. Pope Francis reminds us that they were among the poor and the outcast of their day. Their occupation made them unclean for Temple worship. And yet they were the first to recognize the great gift that had come to earth in this humble stable. Do we recognize the way that gift has transformed our lives?

Your Christmas Gift Today

If you have your Nativity scene set up, take the figures of Mary, Joseph, and the baby away and spend some time praying before the empty manger. Think about what your life might be like if Jesus hadn't been born. Then reflect on all that happened to Jesus after he outgrew that simple manger. What limitations might God be asking you to outgrow?

Knowing We Have Enough

The newborn Child challenges us. He calls us to leave behind fleeting illusions and to turn to what is essential, to renounce our insatiable cravings, to abandon our endless yearning for things we will never have. We do well to leave such things behind, in order to discover, in the simplicity of the divine Child, peace, joy, and the luminous meaning of life.

So when we hear tell of the birth of Christ, let us be silent and let the Child speak. Let us take his words to heart in rapt contemplation of his face. If we take him in our arms and let ourselves be embraced by him, he will bring us unending peace of heart. This Child teaches us what is truly essential in our lives. He was born into the poverty of this world; there was no room in the inn for him and his family. He found shelter and support in a stable and was laid in a manger for animals. And yet, from this nothingness, the light of God's glory shines forth. From now on, the way of authentic liberation and perennial redemption is open to every man and woman who is simple of heart.

A Christmas Reality

If you watch television from Thanksgiving through December, especially during sports events, it seems as though the only appropriate Christmas gift is a diamond or a luxury car. Since I'm not likely to expect or want either one, I roll my eyes. But I wonder how much this colors people's expectations. Do they feel cheated if a Lexus with a bow isn't sitting in the driveway on Christmas morning? Do they feel not quite loved enough if there's no jewelry box under the tree?

It's easy to get caught up in the gift-giving side of Christmas. My mom used to keep a little book where she listed everything she bought for Christmas each year. And she always wanted to make sure each child and grandchild had the same number of packages. Often we go overboard trying to impress someone or trying to make them happy. Sometimes we feel that we have to match gifts given and received. We're afraid that someone might give us a gift and we have nothing for them in return, so we keep little emergency gifts wrapped in the spare room.

Pope Francis reminds us that the incarnation is about the utter simplicity and humility of God becoming human. No jewelry, no fancy transportation, not even a new living room suite. Even the gifts of the magi mattered less for what they were than for what they represented: a child born to be priest, prophet, and king; a child who would die that all people might be saved.

Your Christmas Gift Today

Reflect on Pope Francis saying, "This Child teaches us what is truly essential in our lives." There's a saying that true contentment lies not in having what you want but wanting what you have. Think about ways you can simplify gift-giving with your family and friends, perhaps by focusing on one truly meaningful (but not necessarily expensive) gift.

Overcoming Our Doubts and Insecurities

*T*onight, may we too be challenged and called by Jesus. Let us approach him with trust, starting from all those things that make us feel marginalized, from our limitations and our sins. Let us be touched by the tenderness that saves. Let us draw close to God, who draws close to us. Let us pause to gaze upon the crib, and relive in our imagination the birth of Jesus: light and peace, dire poverty and rejection. With the shepherds, let us enter into the real Christmas, bringing to Jesus all that we are, our alienation, our unhealed wounds, our sins. Then, in Jesus, we will enjoy the taste of the true spirit of Christmas: the beauty of being loved by God. With Mary and Joseph, let us pause before the manger, before Jesus who is born as bread for my life. Contemplating his humble and infinite love, let us simply tell him: Thank you. Thank you because you have done all this for me.

A Christmas Reality

The gifts we give are ultimately about the receiver, not about the giver. How often when we're giving gifts do we think about how the gift will reflect on us, our great taste, our generosity, our discretionary income? Much of this stems from insecurity, a fear that we're somehow not enough in ourselves, that what we do and how much we make and the gifts we give bolster our sense of self. But the peril of this approach is that we're bound to be disappointed by the receiver's reaction, no matter how much they thank us.

The Christmas holidays often surface doubts and insecurities that we ignore the rest of the year. It might be the stress of extra activities, more spending than we're accustomed to, less sleep than we need, more food and drink than we should have. We see people we haven't seen in several months, perhaps not since last Christmas, and we wonder what they think of us. Family gatherings can raise tensions as well.

Pope Francis recognizes that the wonder of the birth of Jesus is balanced by a darker reality: We are all broken and marginalized in some way. He says this not to judge or condemn us but to call us to see the mercy and forgiveness that are such an essential part of the incarnation. The peace we can't find in our daily life is waiting for us in the love of God, a love so clearly shown in the gift of Jesus.

YOUR CHRISTMAS GIFT TODAY

Treat yourself to a little soul-searching. We usually know what fault we most need to work on in ourselves. Minor issues can often be dealt with through some reflection and journaling, being honest with ourselves, and making a commitment to work on our bad habits. More serious issues might need some counseling or therapy. That could be the best Christmas gift you could give yourself. Many churches have special reconciliation services during the Advent season; if you're so inclined, you might want to attend one, with or without individual confession. A peaceful heart is one of the greatest gifts of Christmas.

The Paradox of the Incarnation

A Quiet Reflection from Pope Francis

With this sign, the Gospel reveals a paradox. It speaks of the emperor, the governor, the high and mighty of those times, yet God does not make himself present there. He appears not in the splendor of a royal palace, but in the poverty of a stable; not in pomp and show, but in simplicity of life; not in power, but in astonishing smallness. In order to meet him, we need to go where he is. We need to bow down, to humble ourselves, to make ourselves small.

A Christmas Reality

We live in a world increasingly dominated by celebrities and news of celebrities, no matter how trivial. Perhaps it's always been that way, but our electronic devices give us instant access. The days of the 24/7 cable news channels have been replaced by minute-by-minute updates from Twitter and other social media sites. We're not necessarily better for this deluge of information; it tends to skew our perception of reality. We may know more about our favorite celebrities than we do about our friends or coworkers.

From the very beginning of the Gospels, we see God turning expectations upside down. This is very much in keeping with the story of the Chosen People in the Old Testament. God's choice of favorites has often been from among the insignificant, the unnoticed, the also-rans. Noah, Abraham, Moses, David…no high-society celebrities for our God. And so we come to his own son, born not in a palace but in a stable.

This should give us a clue about where to find God's presence in our world today. We're far more likely to get a glimpse of the divine in the grateful smile of a homeless person, the store clerk grateful for a kind greeting instead of a complaint, or the heartfelt greeting of a dear friend than in news from Hollywood or New York or Washington, D.C. To do this, we need to put ourselves where real life happens: our families, our schools, our work-places, the soup kitchen, the animal shelter. We need to be where people are serving and being served. This is the revelation of the incarnation.

YOUR CHRISTMAS GIFT TODAY

Try to give a simple greeting to each person you see today. It might be looking directly at the person begging at the exit ramp to the interstate, the person at the next gas pump, the hot dog seller in front of the downtown office building, the person at work that you normally don't talk to. For your family and friends, go the extra step of making sure you tell them, "I love you." Life is less about who we are than about how much we love and are loved.

When You Eat and Drink, Remember Me

A Quiet Reflection from Pope Francis

He is born in Bethlehem, which means "house of bread." In this way, he seems to tell us that he is born as bread for us; he enters our life to give us his life; he comes into our world to give us his love. He does not come to devour or to lord it over us, but instead to feed and serve us.

A Christmas Reality

I think my family is pretty typical in that we have a whole category of family recipes that are reserved for the holidays. Christmas cookies, appetizers and dips, and special drink concoctions, all become part of the Christmas experience. In most cases, there's no longer any reason to serve these dishes only once a year.

When I was a child, these were just the foods you ate at Christmas. The older I get, the more I realize that many of the recipes have been handed down from generation to generation. My mom's handwriting on a recipe card brings a smile to my face (and sometimes tears). Food is a ritual part of our lives in so many ways. The taste of a particular food explodes with memories of family and friends.

It's no wonder, then, that when Jesus wanted to be present to his followers after his death he chose bread and wine as the simple forms for that presence, no complicated recipe with exotic ingredients but the staples of life, fruit of the earth, work of human hands, wheat and grapes, bread and wine. His very birth in Bethlehem, the city of King David, begins that association with the bread of life.

Your Christmas Gift Today

Set aside some time to cook one of your family's holiday dishes. See this as an opportunity to enter into spiritual time with loved ones, living and dead. If you have children, make sure they know the story of the first person in the family who made that particular recipe. If your parents or grandparents are alive, invite them over to make the meal with you. If they've passed on, spend the time thinking about them in prayerful communion. Our memories and family ties are the best seasoning for any dish.

Learning Generosity

A Quiet Reflection from Pope Francis

Let us pause before the manger to contemplate how God has been present throughout this year and to remind ourselves that every age, every moment is the bearer of graces and blessings. The manger challenges us not to give up on anything or anyone. To look upon the manger means to find the strength to take our place in history without complaining or being resentful, without closing in on ourselves or seeking a means of escape, looking for shortcuts in our own interest."

A Christmas Reality

Learning to be generous with those who are less fortunate is a lesson that can be taught from our earliest years. As we learn to share within our families and with friends, we can also learn to share with those around us. Often parishes and other organizations have giving trees and collections during the holidays. Many families make a point of taking their children to shop for these gifts, explaining to them why we reach out to others in a special way at this time of year. It gives them an appreciation for what they have and an awareness of our call to care for the least of our brothers and sisters.

While necessities are important, it's lovely to add a few niceties as well. Pope Francis has done a wonderful job of modeling true charity that feeds the heart and soul as well as the body. He's arranged for food, shelter, even showers for Rome's homeless, but he's also had his almoner arrange beach visits, pizza parties, and visits to the Sistine Chapel. Jesus calls us to treat others not only as we would like to be treated, but also as we would do if were serving him.

Your Christmas Gift Today

The familiar Peace Prayer of St. Francis assures us that "it is in giving that we receive." If you haven't already chosen a charity for this Christmas season, make a point of doing so today. There's no shortage of need in our world, and if you like, you can find something that fits your family's interests. This will make it more personal, more of a bond than a cold and impersonal duty. You might want to think about making a commitment to this group through the year. Often we donate or volunteer at the holidays because of special appeals for donations, but the needs aren't limited to one or two months of the year.

Reaching Out in Mercy

*I*t is beautiful that there be present in this manger scene a figure which immediately grasps the mystery of Christmas. It is that character who performs a good deed, bending down to lend a helping hand to an elderly person. He not only looks to God, but also imitates him, because, like God, he bends down with mercy to those in need. May these gifts of yours, which will be illuminated tonight, draw the gaze of many and especially rekindle in life the true light of Christmas.

A Christmas Reality

When I read this reflection from Pope Francis, I immediately wanted to searching for the photo that accompanied the papal audience, because I was intrigued by his description of this figure in the Nativity scene. He has a way of drawing our attention to very human details in the midst of what could easily be a ceremonial blessing. This is part of his gift and grace as pope. He calls us to relate to one another on a very personal level. His acts of mercy and charity go beyond what we might think of as perfunctory or required. One of my favorite pictures of the pope was taken when he celebrated breakfast on his birthday with three homeless men and their dog. So it's not surprising that he would call out a crèche figure helping an elderly person.

Looking to the margins is often where we'll be surprised by a glimpse of God. We become too familiar with the main players in the Gospels. We expect Jesus, Mary, and Joseph to be exemplary role models. But for the Christian message to take root, there must have been hundreds, even thousands, among the early followers of Jesus to live the life he exemplified, to witness to his words with their deeds.

Sometimes seeing someone else offering their service to another person in need is all we need to spark our own mercy and generosity. We think, "That doesn't seem so hard. I could do that." We are called to be generous to others because God has been so very generous to us. We are merciful toward others because we know

God has been merciful to us. We forgive as we have been forgiven or even as we hope to be forgiven. And in turn we become role models for someone else.

The phrase "pay it forward" came into vogue several years ago with a book by that name. The concept is as old as the Gospels, perhaps as old as the human race. It's the bedrock of the values that govern the lives of all religions and most civilizations. We know it as the Golden Rule, the greatest commandment, but really it all comes down to love.

Your Christmas Gift Today

Find a way to surprise someone with a helping hand today. It could be a friend, a family member, a stranger. You might already know what you're going to do. If you don't, pray that God will give you a nudge at the right time. And then keep your eyes open for the opportunity. Chances are you'll find it so rewarding that you'll do it again—and again.

"He Kept Christmas in His Heart"

A Quiet Reflection from Pope Francis

A great and daily attitude of Christian freedom is necessary in order to have the courage to proclaim, in our city, that it is necessary to protect the poor, and not to protect ourselves from the poor, that we must serve the weak and not take advantage of them! The teaching of a simple Roman deacon can help us. When St Lawrence was asked to bring and display the treasures of the Church, he simply brought a few poor people. In a city, when the poor and the weak are cared for, aided and helped to play their part in society, they reveal themselves to be the treasure of the Church and a treasure in the society.

A Christmas Reality

Every year my friends and I have the same conversation: Which is the best film adaptation of *A Christmas Carol*? My favorite will always be the 1983 version with George C. Scott. Perhaps it's because I was going through a conversion experience of my own at that time, returning to my childhood religion with a new adult faith, but I was struck by the conversion element of Dickens's timeless tale.

Through the course of this familiar story, we see Ebenezer Scrooge coming to terms with his past the rejection by his father, the death of his beloved sister, his absorption in the business of making money, and his own rejection of Belle and the chance for a family of his own. Confronted with poverty, ignorance, and want, he first turns away but then comes to realize that change is something in his power to achieve.

The Victorians weren't particularly subtle in their moral teachings. What I find intriguing in Scott's portrayal of the character is an element of humor that in the beginning is sneering and mocking, that descends easily into anger, but later becomes a lighthearted joy that has him, in his own words, feeling "giddy as a schoolboy." This marks a powerful change for someone who was anything but giddy when he was, in fact, a boy alone and lonely at school.

One of the characteristics of Pope Francis's ministry is his emphasis on the deep joy of conversion and evangelization. More than anything else, a life lived by Gospel values is a life of joy and happiness, a life of reaching out to others for the simple pleasure of being connected as human beings and children of God.

Your Christmas Gift Today

Watch your favorite version of *A Christmas Carol* this evening. Pay special attention to the ways in which Scrooge changes, and reflect on what might have caused the change. Ask yourself whether you need to make similar changes in any part of your own life.

Letting Ourselves Be Loved

On this holy night, while we contemplate the Infant Jesus just born and placed in the manger, we are invited to reflect. How do we welcome the tenderness of God? Do I allow myself to be taken up by God, to be embraced by him, or do I prevent him from drawing close? "But I am searching for the Lord"—we could respond. Nevertheless, what is most important is not seeking him, but rather allowing him to seek me, find me and caress me with tenderness. The question put to us simply by the Infant's presence is: do I allow God to love me?

A Christmas Reality

One of the stories in my family is of the time when my mom was trying to teach me the truth that it's more blessed to give than to receive. I may have been six or seven at the time. I happily offered to let other people have the blessing of giving to me while I did the receiving. It was a child's self-absorbed logic, but it's something to consider.

Often we are uncomfortable receiving gifts, particularly if we're not able to match it with a return gift. We want to be the ones acting and giving and doing for others. It appeals to our sense of being capable and independent adults. Pope Francis reminds us yet again that God's gift in the incarnation turns that upside down. God loves us so much that he gave us a gift we can never repay.

If we let ourselves be loved by God, we discover that all our striving and activity is taking us in the wrong direction. We are not our work or our bank account or even our spiritual activities. We are simply loved by God, held in God's embrace. If Christmas can teach us this lesson, our lives will change in ways that we can't even imagine.

Your Christmas Gift Today

Some lessons can only be learned in the quiet of our hearts. But sometimes we have to get there first. There's a line that says "If you're too busy to pray, you're too busy." Set aside an hour for prayer sometime in the next day or two. Begin by simply being quiet, paying attention to your breathing. Feel the stress of the day or the season begin to recede. Focus on simply letting yourself be loved by God. (Note: This is an exercise you can certainly do more than once!)

Those Long-Standing Traditions

A Quiet Reflection from Pope Francis

Today, before the little Child Jesus, we should acknowledge that we need the Lord to enlighten us, because all too often we end up being narrow-minded or prisoners of an all-or-nothing attitude that would force others to conform to our own ideas. We need this light, which helps us learn from our mistakes and failed attempts in order to improve and surpass ourselves; this light born of the humble and courageous awareness of those who find the strength, time and time again, to rise up and start anew.

A Christmas Reality

Is there anything so set in stone as some of our family holiday traditions? I'm sure there are families who take an "anything goes" approach to holiday customs, but I suspect there are a lot more where each sibling has a different idea about what "we've always done"—for meals, for decorating, for family gatherings. This seems to get worse as we get older. We're responsible adults in every other area of our lives but when the family clan gathers, the adult siblings revert to adolescence and birth order and whatever else influences our inability to grow beyond our childhood patterns.

We cling to a past that we may not remember accurately. "But we've always gone to Mom's on Christmas Eve before Midnight Mass." Except "always" might be the last ten years. And now Mom is too old and frail to host that gathering. But we get stuck for alternatives. If we stubbornly cling to having these things our way, the reactions from the rest of the family might range from secretly amused to annoyed to angry. Tensions fray easily at this time of year. Sometimes such issues don't get resolved until parents are gone and we have children of our own and circumstances force a change on us without our having a choice.

The promise of our faith is that of conversion. We can change. Our loved ones can change. We learn, we grow, we move forward. We'll make mistakes along the way, but we learn from them. We forgive and we're forgiven. Even when we're celebrating

Christmas, resurrection is at the heart of our faith. We really can do things differently.

Your Christmas Gift Today

Reflect on whether there's a custom, big or small, to which you're clinging to the point of arguing with others over it. If you can't think of one, ask a brother or sister to suggest one. You might be surprised. Letting go is a process. You might want to look at what you value about the way you've "always" done something. Is there a way to hold on to that while changing some of the details? Maybe letting new family members play a role? Or you might want to come up with a fresh, new alternative. Others may even learn from your flexibility!

Let There Be Light

In turning on the light of the Christmas tree, we wish for the light of Christ to be in us. A Christmas without light is not Christmas. Let there be light in the soul, in the heart; let there be forgiveness to others; let there be no hostilities or darkness.... Let there be the beautiful light of Jesus. This is my wish for all of you, when you turn on the light of the Christmas tree.

I give to you my warmest wishes, peace and happiness. If you have something dark in your soul, ask the Lord for forgiveness. Christmas is a great opportunity to cleanse the soul! Do not fear, the priest is merciful, forgiving all in the name of God, because God forgives everything. May there be light be in your hearts, in your families, in your cities. And now, with this wish, let us turn on the light.

A Christmas Reality

Jesus told us that we're the light of the world, and do we ever take him seriously when we're celebrating his birth! We string lights inside and outside, wrapped around pillars and fences, trailing from rooftops. Now we have laser light shows that play on the front of the house. We string lights in the house around doorways and up and down stairs. The tree might have big lights, little lights, LED lights, bubble lights, and a lighted star at the very top. And no matter how old we get, there's still a little bit of magic when we switch them on.

Our love of light may go all the way back to an ancestral memory, at least in the northern hemisphere, of fearing the darkness and the cold of winter. The twinkling holiday lights give us not so much utilitarian light as a sparkle and dazzle that imitates the stars on a crisp cold night. So it's not surprising that spiritual teachers through the millennia, beginning even before Jesus, have used light as a metaphor for holiness, for joy, for peace.

As researchers study the effect of various kinds of light on the parts of our brain that control waking and sleeping as well as mood disorders, we gain knowledge and insight. People in climates that have long stretches of dark, gray days have learned to use light therapy to keep depression and seasonal affective disorder at bay. But mostly, we're putting a name to what we already know instinctively: Light makes us happy.

YOUR CHRISTMAS GIFT TODAY

Gather your family and friends as darkness falls tonight. If you have decorated your Christmas tree, have a ceremonial lighting of it. If not, you might want to light several candles. Use this blessing from the pope to bring peace and good cheer to those gathered:

> In turning on the light of the Christmas tree,
> we wish for the light of Christ to be in us.
> Let there be light in the soul, in the heart;
> let there be forgiveness to others;
> let there be no hostilities or darkness.
> Let there be the beautiful light of Jesus.
> May there be light be in our hearts, in our families,
>   in our cities.
> And now, with this wish, let us turn on the light.

The Empty Chair

A Quiet Reflection from Pope Francis

The mystery of Christmas, which is light and joy, challenges and unsettles us, because it is at once a mystery of hope and of sadness. It has a taste of sadness, inasmuch as love is not accepted, and life discarded. Christmas has above all a taste of hope because, for all the darkness in our lives, God's light shines forth. His gentle light does not frighten us. God, who is in love with us, draws us to himself with his tenderness, by being born poor and frail in our midst, as one of us.

A Christmas Reality

Perhaps one of the most difficult times we have at Christmas is when we're facing the loss of someone we have dearly loved. It might be a parent, a sibling, a spouse, a child, a grandchild, a very dear friend. If it's someone who was important in our lives, the hole they leave in our hearts can be immense, and it's often magnified still further by the memories that are woven through our Christmas celebrations.

We know with our minds and through our faith that our loved ones are still with us in some way we can't perceive with our human senses. But it's the sight and sound and touch of them that we miss. On this feast, when we celebrate our God taking on our human flesh, we long for the human, bodily reality of those who have died.

In the celebration of Lessons and Carols, the bidding prayer at the beginning speaks of remembering "those who rejoice with us but on another shore and in a greater light." This recollection gives us some degree of comfort, although nothing can take away all the sadness. And perhaps we wouldn't want it to. The very sadness that we feel, the tears that we cry, are proof that we have loved and been loved. It's a bittersweet mystery. And some would say that our incarnate God who loves us weeps with us in these times of loss.

YOUR CHRISTMAS GIFT TODAY

Take some quiet time to think about someone dearly loved and now lost to earthly sight. It might be a recent loss or one that has recently resurfaced. Grief has no solid boundaries of time and space. You might want to look through a photo album, listen to a favorite piece of music, or find some other way to let your emotions surface. As you do, let yourself feel the tenderness of God embracing you, weeping with you, bringing light to the dark places in your heart.

Light in the Darkness

*I*saiah's prophecy announces the rising of a great light which breaks through the night. This light is born in Bethlehem and is welcomed by the loving arms of Mary, by the love of Joseph, by the wonder of the shepherds. When the angels announced the birth of the Redeemer to the shepherds, they did so with these words: "This will be a sign for you: you will find a baby wrapped in swaddling clothes and lying in a manger" (Luke 2:12). The "sign" is in fact the humility of God, the humility of God taken to the extreme; it is the love with which, that night, he assumed our frailty, our suffering, our anxieties, our desires and our limitations. The message that everyone was expecting, that everyone was searching for in the depths of their souls, was none other than the tenderness of God: God who looks upon us with eyes full of love, who accepts our poverty, God who is in love with our smallness. We too, in this blessed night, have come to the house of God. We have passed through the darkness which envelops the earth, guided by the flame of faith which illuminates our steps, and enlivened by the hope of finding the "great light." By opening our hearts, we also can contemplate the miracle of that child-sun who, arising from on high, illuminates the horizon.

A Christmas Reality

We do our brothers and sisters, perhaps even ourselves, a great disservice at Christmastime if we pretend that the holidays are all sweetness and light, sugar plums and gift-giving, happy families and peaceful hearts. Because pretense it would be. The holidays can be extremely difficult for people for myriad reasons. The loss of loved ones, loneliness, mental health issues, being far away from family, and working long hours in jobs that don't slow down because it's Christmas are just a few that come to mind. In many ways the worst thing about feeling lost in the darkness is the belief that everyone around us is enjoying the bright lights, the happy music, the united families, and all the rest. The loneliness and isolation can compound the sadness.

The prophet Isaiah, whom Pope Francis quotes here, is the most consistent voice through the Advent and Christmas season. And he speaks most eloquently to those who are lost in the dark. He preached to the people of Israel in the eighth century BC, when most of them were exiled in Babylon, far from their homes. He knew about people who walk in darkness.

The hope offered by the Scriptures, highlighted here by Pope Francis, is no easy-but-empty promise that there are brighter days ahead. It's a deep, heartfelt belief that God's light can penetrate the most profound darkness. It's a hope we can cling to in the dark, in the silence, in the loneliness. We are blessed if we have people who stay with us in these difficult times when words fail and all seems lost. And we know that for some, God's great light won't break upon their darkness in this world. But we believe that one day all will surely walk in that light.

Your Christmas Gift Today

Light a candle today for all those who are walking in some kind of darkness during this Christmas season. Pray for the strength to walk with them, to be the support they need. Above all, pray that they will be held in God's loving embrace. When our own strength fails, when we feel inadequate in the face of another's suffering, we turn them, and ourselves, over to a loving and merciful God.

The Power of Love

Today the Church once more experiences the wonder of the Blessed Virgin Mary, Saint Joseph and the shepherds of Bethlehem, as they contemplate the newborn Child laid in a manger: Jesus, the Savior. On this day full of light, the prophetic proclamation resounds:

> For to us a child is born,
> To us a son is given.
> And the government will be upon his shoulder;
> and his name will be called
> "Wonderful Counselor, Mighty God,
> Everlasting Father, Prince of Peace." (Isaiah 9:6)

The power of this Child, Son of God and Son of Mary, is not the power of this world, based on might and wealth; it is the power of love. It is the power that created the heavens and the earth, and gives life to all creation: to minerals, plants and animals. It is the force that attracts man and woman, and makes them one flesh, one single existence. It is the power that gives new birth, forgives sin, reconciles enemies, and transforms evil into good. It is the power of God. This power of love led Jesus Christ to strip himself of his glory and become man; it led him to give his life on the cross and to rise from the dead. It is the power of service, which inaugurates in our world the Kingdom of God, a kingdom of justice and peace.

A CHRISTMAS REALITY

We've been reflecting on the many ways in which our lives during the holidays mirror and are mirrored by the Scriptures and our faith in the incarnation. We understand the tenderness and sweetness of our God coming to us as a newborn child. We understand the metaphors of light and warmth. We know the convivial joy of holiday parties and sharing good food and drink. But sometimes we need to take a step back from our holiday traditions, our family activities, our cultural customs, and feel the real power of what Christmas can be in our lives, in our families, in our world.

We struggle for peace in so many ways, large and small. Sometimes the holidays can seem artificial. Sometimes all our efforts seem inadequate. Today's words from Isaiah and from Pope Francis are a not-so-quiet reflection. They are a wake-up call to hear, to believe, to know in our heart of hearts that God is greater than any problem we have. And the source and manifestation of that divine power is love. We may only feel the full strength of that kind of love a few precious times in our lives. But once we've felt it, we never completely forget it. Again and again in the Bible we hear that God is love. The feast of Christmas challenges us to believe that and then to show it forth in the way we live our lives.

Your Christmas Gift Today

Attend a performance in your area of Handel's Messiah. If there's none being held near you, listen to one of the many recorded versions. Let the power of the music carry the words of Scripture into the depths of your being. Music can open our bodies and souls to an awareness of truth in a way that spoken words alone cannot always achieve.

Seeing with the Eyes of God

*L*et us imagine how our world would change if each of us started immediately, here and now, to take proper care of our relationship with God and with our neighbor; if we put into practice the golden rule of the Gospel, Jesus proposed in the Sermon on the Mount: "whatever you wish that men would do to you, do so to them; for this is the law and the prophets" (Mathew 7:12). If only we could look at others, especially the most needy, with eyes of goodness and tenderness, as God looks at us, awaits us and forgives us; if we could find in humility our strength and our treasure! And so often we are afraid of tenderness, we are afraid of humility!

A Christmas Reality

There's a man I see frequently near our post office selling a newspaper for one of the homeless coalitions in town. He has limited sight and limited resources, but he always has a smile and a kind word for anyone who passes. When I ask him how he is, he usually answers with a smile, "Better than some; worse than others." I always feel better for encountering him. And he has the perspective we all could take, because aren't each of us better than some and worse than others?

Christmas offers us many opportunities to care for those less fortunate than ourselves. It's a good way to keep the creeping excesses of the season from getting out of hand. Pope Francis certainly never lets us forget that there are many people in the world who need what we can offer them. Here he refers to it as seeing everyone with the eyes of God. God offers us the mercy, the forgiveness, the love that we need. How can we not offer the same to others in our turn?

Your Christmas Gift Today

Make a God's Eye ornament for the tree (instructions can be found online) or make several to use as tags on packages for your loved ones. Let them be a reminder to see ourselves and those around us with the eyes of God.

The Challenge of Christmas

*L*et us allow the Child in the manger to challenge us, but let us also be challenged by all those children in today's world who are lying not in a crib, caressed with affection by their mothers and fathers, but in squalid "mangers that devour dignity." Children who hide underground to escape bombardment, on the pavements of large cities, in the hold of a boat overladen with immigrants.... Let us allow ourselves to be challenged by those children who are not allowed to be born, by those who cry because no one relieves their hunger, by those who hold in their hands not toys, but weapons.

In the face of little Jesus, we contemplate the face of God, who does not reveal himself in strength and power but in the weakness and frailty of a newborn babe. This is what our God is like, he comes so close, in a child. This Child reveals the faithfulness and tenderness of the unconditional love with which God surrounds each one of us. That is why we celebrate at Christmas, thus reliving what the shepherds at Bethlehem experienced. And we celebrate together with so many fathers and mothers who struggle each day, facing so many sacrifices; we celebrate together with the little ones, the sick, the poor, for it is the celebration of God's encounter with us in Jesus.

A CHRISTMAS REALITY

We often say that Christmas is for children, and indeed there's something precious about watching young children experience the joy and wonder of the lights and decorations and presents under the tree. But Pope Francis does well to remind us that not all children experience these things that so many of us take for granted. Often we can't even imagine how terrible life is for these children.

This is the challenge of the Gospel, the challenge of Jesus. That challenge doesn't go away because it's Christmas. We don't get a break from the reality of suffering and violence in our world. To hide our faces is to compound our guilt. Pope Francis never tires of telling us that our God is merciful and loving, filled with tender love and forgiveness. But that love comes at a price. For Jesus, it was the cross. For us, it's knowing that we need to be the care and protection of God to all people, especially those who are suffering the most.

If we want to see Jesus this Christmas, the best place to look is in the faces of the least ones, the lost ones, the suffering ones. As individuals, we can never do enough. But we can't let that keep us from doing what we can. Only then can we look to our own happiness and peace.

Your Christmas Gift Today

Children are suffering all over the world from war, from the refugee crisis, from human trafficking, from poverty, from abuse. Lest you think it's only a problem in developing countries, many agencies in your own city will tell you that children are suffering close to home as well. Find some way to get involved in helping to alleviate this problem. Even a small step is a good beginning. Do it for them, do it out of gratitude for the joy-filled children in your own family, do it for the God who became one of us and risked his life as a small and vulnerable child.

The Whole World Being at Peace

*L*et us open our hearts to receive the grace of this day, which is Christ himself. Jesus is the radiant "day" which has dawned on the horizon of humanity. A day of mercy, in which God our Father has revealed his great tenderness to the entire world. A day of light, which dispels the darkness of fear and anxiety. A day of peace, which makes for encounter, dialogue and, above all, reconciliation. A day of joy: a "great joy" for the poor, the lowly and for all the people (see Luke 2:10). The grace of God can convert hearts and offer mankind a way out of humanly insoluble situations. Where God is born, hope is born. He brings hope. Where God is born, peace is born. And where peace is born, there is no longer room for hatred and for war. True peace—we know this well—is not a balance of opposing forces. It is not a lovely "façade" which conceals conflicts and divisions. Peace calls for daily commitment, but making peace is an art, starting from God's gift, from the grace which he has given us in Jesus Christ.

A Christmas Reality

The Church's traditional proclamation of the feast of Christmas, normally read at the Mass at Midnight, puts the birth of Jesus in the context of all of history and indeed all of time from the creation of the world. As it moves through prehistory to the history of the Greek and Roman empires in the last centuries before Jesus was born, it builds to the climax of "the whole world being at peace." And in that one moment in time, Christ was incarnate in the person of Jesus. But we know that, in fact, the whole world was not at peace. Jesus was born into an occupied territory. And the world has never been entirely at peace since. But in our faith, we still have hope for that peace.

In November 2015, shortly after the terrorist bombings in Paris, Pope Francis suggested that Christmas that year would be merely a charade because the whole world was at war. As with many things Pope Francis says and does, the news traveled fast. But we didn't have a year without a Christmas. Our pope knows that the world, like all of us who make up its population, is still in need of forgiveness and salvation. The process that began with the birth of a vulnerable child in Bethlehem continues today, and we are called to be part of bringing that peace about.

On Christmas and Easter each year, the pope delivers an address known in Latin as the *Urbi et Orbi* (the City and the World). He intercedes in a special way for all the troubled places around the globe, for all the ways in which people still suffer at the hands of others. He calls on God for protection, for liberation, for salvation. And he calls on those of us who follow Christ to do our part.

This, too, is the reality of Christmas, and we need to make it part of our awareness if we're going to find wholeness and peace now and in the year ahead.

Your Christmas Gift Today

Peace begins in the heart and moves outward. If we're not at peace within ourselves, conflict will find its way into our daily interactions with others. If our families and neighborhoods are not at peace, turmoil in our cities will spread. As we move toward the new year, make a commitment to focus on peace through prayer, through meditation, through working for justice.

The Wonder of an Infant

*Y*ou will find a child wrapped in swaddling clothes and lying in a manger" (Luke 2:12). This is the enduring sign for all who would find Jesus. Not just then, but also today. If we want to celebrate Christmas authentically, we need to contemplate this sign: the frail simplicity of a tiny newborn child, the meekness with which he is placed in a manger, the tender affection with which he is wrapped in his swaddling clothes. That is where God is.

A Christmas Reality

At family gatherings this time of year, nothing gives more joy than the smallest baby in the family being passed around, held, and cuddled. This tiny bundle of life delights old and young alike. New parents understand the Christmas story in a way that no one else can. It's easy to see God in the face of a newborn.

Again and again Pope Francis returns to the simplicity and the vulnerability of baby Jesus. We know how fragile newborn life can be. And we know that these tiny lives can still be lost, even with all the technological advances of our own century. But we also believe that God holds these little ones in his hands, even when we can't. Our children's lives are incredibly precious to us, no matter how old we are or how long or short a time they live. I recently watched a ninety-eight-year-old woman mourn the death of her son with as much grief as the mother of a newborn or the mother of a young adult. Our children are always our children. And all of them are God's children and fiercely loved by their divine parent.

If you have infants or small children in your family or among your friends, take time to delight in them in a special way during this Christmas season. And hold in prayer all those who have lost children and all those whose children suffer in dire circumstances.

Your Christmas Gift Today

Find a special "Baby's First Christmas" ornament for an infant you know. This is something that will be cherished by the parents and then the children themselves for years to come. At the same time, find a local organization that cares for families in need and make a donation of diapers, formula, and other things that all infants need.

A Time for Family

Let us remember that the most precious gifts for children are not things but their parents' love. I do not mean only the parents' love for their children, but the parents' own love between themselves, which is the conjugal relationship. This does such good for you and also for your children! Do not overlook your family! Speak with your children, listen to them, ask them what they think. This dialogue between parents and children does so much good! It makes the children grow in maturity. Let us focus on mercy, in everyday relationships, between husband and wife, between parents and children, between brothers and sisters; and let's take care of grandparents: grandparents are so important in the family. Grandparents have memories, they have wisdom. Never leave grandparents aside! They are very important. A young woman—who has a seven-year-old son and whose ninety-year-old grandmother lives with them—told me that the grandmother was not completely well and they advised that she be admitted to a rest home. This wise woman, who had not studied at university, replied to those who told her to put her grandmother in a rest home: "No! I want my son to grow up beside his grandma!" She knew the good that grandparents do for their grandchildren.

A CHRISTMAS REALITY

We're familiar with the Christmas stories from the Bible that tell us about the birth of the baby in the stable, the visit from the shepherds, the angels singing in the skies, the star that the wise men followed. The Gospel we rarely hear is read at the vigil Mass early in the evening on Christmas Eve. It gives Matthew's account of the genealogy of Jesus. He carefully traces fourteen generations from the call of Abraham to King David, fourteen generations from King David to the Babylonian Exile, and fourteen generations from the Exile to Joseph, who took the pregnant Mary into his home. Few of us today have that kind of passion for tracing our ancestors, but we all have stories passed down in our families from generation to generation. And it's the stories that remind us of who we are and where we came from.

The Church celebrates the feast of the Holy Family in between Christmas and New Year's Day. It's an important reminder that Jesus was born into a human family, that he had parents and grandparents, aunts and uncles and cousins. Pope Francis frequently comments on the importance of extended families and, in particular, the wisdom of the elders in our families. They are often the keepers of the stories. Their experience of the ups and downs of life can be invaluable when we find ourselves struggling with work, with relationships, with raising children.

YOUR CHRISTMAS GIFT TODAY

When your family gathers during the holidays, or perhaps in the slower days of January after things settle down, find time to speak to the older generation in your own family. Use a digital recorder or paper and pen to capture their stories and wisdom before it's too late.

When Our Families Don't Seem So Holy

Through the course of history, the light that shatters the darkness reveals to us that God is Father and that his patient fidelity is stronger than darkness and corruption. This is the message of Christmas night. God does not know outbursts of anger or impatience; he is always there, like the father in the parable of the prodigal son, waiting to catch from afar a glimpse of the lost son as he returns; and every day, with patience. The patience of God.

A CHRISTMAS REALITY

In the 1970s, folk singer John Denver released an album called *Rocky Mountain Christmas*. One of the tracks on it was called "Please, Daddy, Don't Get Drunk This Christmas." My oldest sister, who was a big fan, complained to my mom that it wasn't a Christmas song and didn't belong on a Christmas album. She wasn't living at home anymore. Fourteen years younger, I was in grade school, and my dad's alcoholism had progressed to a point where it was a near constant disruption to our family life. For me, that song expressed a Christmas wish deeper than anything I might put on my list of hoped-for presents.

Sometimes family life doesn't fit the storybook images we all want to see during the holidays. Anger, addiction, separation, and divorce are just a few of the burdens that can strain families and make Christmas anything but peace on earth, goodwill to all. Our relationship with our parents can influence even our understanding of God. This is what makes the pope's description of God the Father particularly poignant. Without saying it in so many words, he's showing us that God can be for us the parent we may have wished we had.

The Feast of the Holy Family can make all of us feel like somehow our lives and relationships fall short. But Pope Francis reminds us that the ideal is always worth working for and struggling toward. Our faith assures us that reconciliation and healing are always options. People can change, circumstances can improve, and we can find ways of working through the difficult times with prayer and the support of loving and caring family and friends.

Your Christmas Gift Today

Most, perhaps all, families struggle with problems large and small. Sometimes we might be tempted to think that the whole concept of family is deeply flawed. But it's the way our relationships have been structured since the beginning of civilization. The specifics might change, but we are social creatures, and we are bonded in parent-child-sibling relationships, for better or for worse. Give thanks for the family that you have; say a prayer for the changes you would like to see. Then reach out to at least one person in your immediate or extended family and simply say, "I'm glad we're family."

Mary, Mother of God

*M*ary treasured all these things and pondered them in her heart!" (Luke 2:19). In these words, Luke describes the attitude with which Mary took in all that they had experienced in those days. Far from trying to understand or master the situation, Mary is the woman who can treasure, that is to say, protect and guard in her heart, the passage of God in the life of his people. Deep within, she had learned to listen to the heartbeat of her Son, and that in turn taught her, throughout her life, to discover God's heartbeat in history. She learned how to be a mother, and in that learning process she gave Jesus the beautiful experience of knowing what it is to be a Son. In Mary, the eternal Word not only became flesh, but also learned to recognize the maternal tenderness of God. With Mary, the God-Child learned to listen to the yearnings, the troubles, the joys and the hopes of the people of the promise. With Mary, he discovered himself a Son of God's faithful people.

Mothers, even at the worst times, are capable of testifying to tenderness, unconditional self-sacrifice and the strength of hope. I have learned much from those mothers whose children are in prison, or lying in hospital beds, or in bondage to drugs, yet, come cold or heat, rain or draught, never stop fighting for what is best for them. Or those mothers who in refugee camps, or even the midst of war, unfailingly embrace and support their children's sufferings. Mothers who literally give their lives so that none of their children will perish. Where there is a mother, there is unity, there is belonging, belonging as children.

A CHRISTMAS REALITY

I'm fascinated by this reflection on Mary and mothers because Pope Francis celebrates the deep bond between mother and child without falling into an unrealistic idealization of the relationship. Even in this most perfect parent-child relationship imaginable, we see a pattern of growth and learning, of a deepening under-standing and sympathy not only of each other but of all people in the world. This is the reflection of a pastor who has spent long hours with families in the best and worst of situations. And he reminds us that Mary herself was a refugee mother, that her son was executed as a criminal.

I've known many people who have difficult relationships with their mothers, even with deep love on both sides.

Your Christmas Gift Today

If your mother is still living, give her a call today. If she's not, use your prayer time to tell her the things you would say if she were still here with you.

As the Year Draws to a Close

As another year draws to an end, let us pause before the manger and express our gratitude to God for all the signs of his generosity in our life and our history, seen in countless ways through the witness of those people who quietly took a risk. A gratitude that is no sterile nostalgia or empty recollection of an idealized and disembodied past, but a living memory, one that helps to generate personal and communal creativity because we know that God is with us. God is with us.

Today the Word of God introduces us in a special way, to the meaning of time, to understand that time is not a reality extrinsic to God, simply because he chose to reveal himself and to save us in history. The meaning of time, temporality, is the atmosphere of God's epiphany, namely, of the manifestation of God's mystery and of his concrete love.

A Christmas Reality

Whether it's the Christmas story in church, the family stories we tell around holiday tables and in gatherings with old friends, or the Christmas movies we watch each year, there's something about the telling of familiar stories that holds a special magic. The young sometimes roll their eyes when Grandma tells the same story every year, and not everyone appreciates the rhythm of the lectionary selections. But this is part of who we are as a family and as a people of God. Life finds its meaning in the stories we tell.

We're approaching the end of the Christmas season. Soon we will back to the ordinary routines of our life. But if we have celebrated the feast of the incarnation well, our lives will be changed. We don't know what the new year will hold for us, for our families, for the world. But we know that God will continue to be with us. As we look back at the significant events of the past year, both the joys and the sorrows, the highs and the lows, we can see how God has shaped us and strengthened us for what lies ahead.

Your Christmas Gift Today

Read your favorite Christmas story from the Bible. For some, it's the story of the shepherds and their flocks; for others, it's the exotic tale of visitors from the East. For still others, it's the grand design in the prologue to John's Gospel. Take time to write out one special Christmas memory.

A Flight into Egypt

The Nativity scene in Saint Peter's Square, created by artist Manwel Grech of Gozo, portrays the Maltese countryside, and integrates the traditional Maltese cross and the luzzu, a typical Maltese sea vessel, which also recalls the sad and tragic reality of seafaring migrants making their way toward Italy. In the painful experience of these brothers and sisters, we are reminded that at the moment of baby Jesus' birth, he found no shelter at the inn and instead was born in a stable in Bethlehem. He was later taken to Egypt to escape the threat of Herod. Those who visit this Nativity scene will be invited to rediscover its symbolic value, which is a message of fraternity, sharing, welcome and solidarity. Nativity scenes in churches, homes and many public places are also an invitation to make room in our lives and in society for

God, hidden in the faces of so many people confronting hardship, poverty and suffering.

A CHRISTMAS REALITY

The Holy Family were refugees from a corrupt political situation and an unstable ruler. No matter how much Matthew focuses on the way this flight into another country fulfilled passages in the Hebrew Scriptures, the fact is they were fleeing for their lives. Pope Francis never misses an opportunity to remind us of this reality. In caring for today's refugees from the many war-torn places around the globe, we are caring for the least of God's people, and the end of Matthew's Gospel reminds us that in doing so, we are caring for Christ himself.

We may wish that our religious experience could take place in some sort of bubble, protected from the political divisions and ideological arguments that blare into our lives from the media. But Jesus was clearly born into a world of politics and ideology, of power struggles and armed conflicts. We can learn from him that our loyalty is ultimately to the kingdom of God and to the truth, not to any one political point of view.

Your Christmas Gift Today

Pray today for a particular part of the world that is experiencing war and upheaval. Learn about the roots of the conflict and what aid organizations are doing to help the innocent victims of the conflict. Pray to the Holy Family to watch in a special way over today's refugees that they might find a place of safety and peace and perhaps one day return to their homes and families.

Follow the Star

Longing for God draws us out of our iron-clad isolation, which makes us think that nothing can change. Longing for God shatters our dreary routines and impels us to make the changes we want and need. Longing for God has its roots in the past yet does not remain there: it reaches out to the future. Believers who feel this longing are led by faith to seek God, as the Magi did, in the most distant corners of history, for they know that there the Lord awaits them. They go to the peripheries, to the frontiers, to places not yet evangelized, to encounter their Lord. Nor do they do this out of a sense of superiority, but rather as beggars who cannot ignore the eyes of those who for whom the Good News is still uncharted territory.

The Magi experienced longing; they were tired of the usual fare. They were all too familiar with, and weary of, the Herods of their own day. But there, in Bethlehem, was a promise of newness, of gratuitousness. There something new was taking place. The Magi were able to worship, because they had the courage to set out. And as they fell to their knees before the small, poor and vulnerable Infant, the unexpected and unknown Child of Bethlehem, they discovered the glory of God.

A Christmas Reality

We often think of the Feast of Epiphany as an exotic story of travelers in the desert—magi, astrologers, men from foreign lands in strange and elaborate costumes, riding camels and elephants and carrying treasures from the Orient. But as Pope Francis points out, while their culture and background might be different than ours, the longing in their hearts is something we know all too well. It's the longing for something to believe, something that will assure us that we're on the right path, that we're following the right star.

I love going out in the yard in the winter to look at the stars. The clear, cold air makes them seem brighter. Different stars are visible in the winter than at other times of the year. As the constellations wheel overhead, there's a sense of vast possibility in the universe, but also a sense of permanence. The sun, the moon, the stars, and our own earth travel through time and space but there's nothing random about those movements. Each has an orbit, an appointed path to travel.

Our lives, too, have an appointed path. We move through the seasons of the year, and the seasons of a lifetime. Sometimes it seems as though the only constant is constant change. But the eternal feasts of the Christmas season remind us that the eternal keeps our feet grounded on the earth and our eyes fixed on God's star, the plan God has for each of our lives.

Your Christmas Gift Today

Take some time this week on a cloudless night to watch the stars, alone or with someone close to you. Reflect on the journeys that might lie ahead in the coming year, whether traveling to a new place or exploring the inner depths of your soul. Ask to be reminded that God journeys with you each time you see the stars in the night sky.

Arise, Shine, Go Forth

Like the Magi, countless people, in our own day, have a "restless heart" which continues to seek without finding sure answers—it is the restlessness of the Holy Spirit that stirs in hearts. They too are looking for a star to show them the path to Bethlehem.

How many stars there are in the sky! And yet the Magi followed a new and different star, which for them shone all the more brightly. They had long peered into the great book of the heavens, seeking an answer to their questions—they had restless hearts—and at long last the light appeared. That star changed them. It made them leave their daily concerns behind and set out immediately on a journey. They listened to a voice deep within, which led them to follow that light. It was the voice of the Holy Spirit, who works in all people. The star guided them, until they found the King of the Jews in a humble dwelling in Bethlehem.

The light which streams from the face of Christ, full of mercy and fidelity. And once we have found him, let us worship him with all our heart, and present him with our gifts: our freedom, our understanding and our love. True wisdom lies concealed in the face of this Child. It is here, in the simplicity of Bethlehem, that the life of the Church is summed up. For here is the wellspring of that light which draws to itself every individual in the world and guides the journey of the peoples along the path of peace.

A Christmas Reality

I once thought I was going to have to move away from family and friends and everyone I knew just weeks before Christmas. It was a startling thought and I wasn't sure how I felt about it. But I believed that God would be with me and that Christmas would still happen that year, that what mattered wasn't all the customs and decorations and family gatherings, but the intimate presence of a God who became one of us.

We've become a very mobile culture, often moving several times in the course of a career. It can be daunting to leave one place for another, to make new friends and build new routines and traditions. But it offers tremendous opportunities to share our gifts in ever-widening circles.

As the Christmas season draws to a close, we reflect not so much on the birth of Jesus as on the impact that birth had on all those who heard of it—the shepherds, the magi, the villagers, and us. We get so busy at this time of year with all the activity that sometimes we forget that this baby whose birth we celebrate was in fact the divine in our midst. The Feast of Epiphany makes clear that by taking on our human reality, God shows us how to move beyond our ordinary routines into lives that can make a difference in our world.

The coming of the Magi to visit the holy family was a sign that Christ had come not only for the people of Bethlehem and Jerusalem but for all people in all times and places. It is a reminder that we're called to be ever more inclusive, to be open to questions from all those who seek the love and the mercy and the peace of God.

Your Christmas Gift Today

Spend some time learning about another religion or another culture, and how they celebrate the presence of God. Often the best thing about growing in knowledge and understanding of others is what it reveals about our own beliefs and the richness of our own traditions.

Our Life Is a Journey

The destiny of every person is symbolized in this journey of the Magi of the East: our life is a journey, illuminated by the lights which brighten our way, to find the fullness of truth and love which we Christians recognize in Jesus, the Light of the World. Like the Magi, every person has two great "books" which provide the signs to guide this pilgrimage: the book of creation and the book of sacred Scripture. What is important is that we be attentive, alert, and listen to God who speaks to us, who always speaks to us. As the Psalm says in referring to the Law of the Lord: "Your word is a lamp to my feet and a light to my path" (Psalm 119:105). Listening to the Gospel, reading it, meditating on it and making it our spiritual nourishment especially allows us to encounter the living Jesus, to experience him and his love.

A Christmas Reality

Our holiday celebrations often keep us indoors. In northern climates, this might be partly because the cold and snowy weather makes going outside a difficult and even unpleasant experience. We hurry from house to car and then into another warm house. In warm climates, the heat finds us scurrying between air conditioned buildings.

Pope Francis reminds us that creation—including the weather—is a gift to be celebrated, not something simply to be controlled and altered. We lose our sense of wonder in nature when we become too absorbed in the structures of everyday life. Most of us have jobs and other responsibilities that keep us indoors.

The people of the Bible lived much closer to the land than we do today. Navigating by the stars was something they did as a matter of course. Jesus's parables reflect a deep knowledge of flocks, fields, and fishing. We can understand these stories better if we grow in our awareness of creation. Pope Francis, like his namesake, St. Francis of Assisi, calls us to read God's presence not only in our holy books but in the holiness of the world around us, plant and animal as well as human.

Your Christmas Gift Today

Spend time outdoors today. If you have children or pets, let them show you how to enjoy the simplest pleasures of being present to nature in all its glory. Reflect on the way the presence of God is revealed in the sky, the trees, the birds and animals. When you return to the house, settle in with a hot or cold beverage and read Psalm 104.

Returning to Nazareth

*A*t the end of that pilgrimage, Jesus returned to Nazareth and was obedient to his parents (see Luke 2:51). This image also contains a beautiful teaching about our families. A pilgrimage does not end when we arrive at our destination, but when we return home and resume our everyday lives, putting into practice the spiritual fruits of our experience.

A Christmas Reality

No matter how much we try to extend the holiday with traveling and vacation time and a last party or two, there comes a time when we need to return to our daily activities and responsibilities. School starts up again, work beckons, and we have to bid farewell to Christmas once again. It can be refreshing to reclaim the space that was filled with the Christmas tree and other decorations. We forsake the Christmas cookies and boxes of candy for healthier food choices in the new year. If we've traveled to visit family, we return home, put away the suitcases, finish vacation laundry, and settle into our lives.

Mary, Joseph, and Jesus traveled a great deal during the first years after the birth—back and forth to Jerusalem, a sojourn in Egypt, a return to their home in Nazareth. And in later years, Luke's Gospel tells us, they traveled on pilgrimage to Jerusalem, where Jesus was separated from his parents and found conversing with holy teachers in the temple.

Perhaps we're a bit relieved that Christmas is over for another year. But perhaps we discover that something has changed in us because of an encounter, a gift, a new insight into the meaning of the incarnation. We can keep a little bit of that with us through the coming year and let it bring light and peace to our everyday lives. Our journey with God doesn't end with the Christmas season. Jesus is forever, not just for Christmas.

Your Christmas Gift Today

As you begin to pack away the decorations for another year, take time to recall your favorite experience of this year. It might be a small moment that nearly went unnoticed or it might be a special occasion or event in your life or the life of someone you love.

As you discard any broken ornaments, burned-out lights or empty boxes, let go of one hurt feeling that may linger from this year's celebrations.

Sources

The Gift of Gratitude
HOLY MASS FOR THE MARIAN DAY ON THE OCCASION OF THE YEAR OF
FAITH, Saint Peter's Square, Sunday, 13 October 2013

The God of Surprises
POPE FRANCIS, MORNING MEDITATION IN THE CHAPEL OF THE DOMUS
SANCTAE MARTHAE, Monday, 20 January 2014

Making a List and Checking It Twice
MEETING WITH THE PERSONNEL OF THE HOLY SEE AND OF THE VATICAN
CITY STATE WITH THEIR FAMILIES, Paul VI Audience Hall, Thursday, 22
December 2016

Balancing Expectations
PRESENTATION OF THE CHRISTMAS GREETINGS TO THE ROMAN CURIA,
Clementine Hall, Monday, 22 December 2014

Christmas Is for Children
GENERAL AUDIENCE, Wednesday, 30 December 2015

Creator of the Stars of Night
ADDRESS OF HIS HOLINESS POPE FRANCIS TO THE DONORS OF THE CRIB
AND THE CHRISTMAS TREE IN ST. PETER'S SQUARE, Paul VI Audience Hall,
Friday, 9 December 2016

Emmanuel—God with Us
MIDNIGHT MASS SOLEMNITY OF THE NATIVITY OF THE LORD, Vatican
Basilica, Saturday, 24 December 2016

The Woman at the Heart of the Christmas Story
HOMILY OF HOLY FATHER FRANCIS FOR THE MARIAN DAY ON THE
OCCASION OF THE YEAR OF FAITH, Saint Peter's Square, Sunday, 13 October
2013

What Do Our Decorations Say?
ADDRESS OF HIS HOLINESS POPE FRANCIS TO THE DELEGATIONS FROM VERONA AND CATANZARO FOR THE GIFT OF THE CRIB AND THE CHRISTMAS TREE IN ST. PETER'S SQUARE, Clementine Hall, Friday, 19 December 2014

It Started with St. Francis
ADDRESS OF HIS HOLINESS POPE FRANCIS TO THE DELEGATIONS FROM TRENTO AND BAVARIA FOR THE GIFT OF THE CRIB AND THE CHRISTMAS TREE IN ST. PETER'S SQUARE, Paul VI Audience Hall, Friday, 18 December 2015

Keeping Christmas Simple
ADDRESS OF HIS HOLINESS POPE FRANCIS TO THE DELEGATIONS FROM TRENTO AND BAVARIA FOR THE GIFT OF THE CRIB AND THE CHRISTMAS TREE IN ST. PETER'S SQUARE, Paul VI Audience Hall, Friday, 18 December 2015

Generations of Ornaments
ADDRESS OF HIS HOLINESS POPE FRANCIS TO THE DELEGATIONS FROM TRENTO AND BAVARIA FOR THE GIFT OF THE CRIB AND THE CHRISTMAS TREE IN ST. PETER'S SQUARE, Paul VI Audience Hall, Friday, 18 December 2015

The Crib and the Cross
MIDNIGHT MASS SOLEMNITY OF THE NATIVITY OF THE LORD, Vatican Basilica, Saturday, 24 December 2016

Knowing We Have Enough
MIDNIGHT MASS SOLEMNITY OF THE NATIVITY OF THE LORD, Vatican Basilica, Saturday, 24 December 2016

Overcoming Our Doubts and Insecurities
MIDNIGHT MASS SOLEMNITY OF THE NATIVITY OF THE LORD, Vatican Basilica, Saturday, 24 December 2016

The Paradox of the Incarnation
MIDNIGHT MASS SOLEMNITY OF THE NATIVITY OF THE LORD, Vatican Basilica, Saturday, 24 December 2016

When You Eat and Drink, Remember Me
MIDNIGHT MASS SOLEMNITY OF THE NATIVITY OF THE LORD, Vatican
Basilica, Saturday, 24 December 2016

Learning Generosity
FIRST VESPERS ON THE SOLEMNITY OF MARY, MOTHER OF GOD AND TE
DEUM IN THANKSGIVING FOR THE PAST YEAR, Vatican Basilica, Saturday, 31
December 2016

Reaching Out in Mercy
ADDRESS OF HIS HOLINESS POPE FRANCIS TO THE DELEGATIONS FROM
TRENTO AND BAVARIA FOR THE GIFT OF THE CRIB AND THE CHRISTMAS
TREE IN ST. PETER'S SQUARE, Paul VI Audience Hall, Friday, 18 December 2015

"He Kept Christmas in His Heart"
TE DEUM AND CELEBRATION OF FIRST VESPERS OF THE SOLEMNITY OF
MARY, MOTHER OF GOD, Vatican Basilica, Wednesday, 31 December 2014

Letting Ourselves Be Loved
MIDNIGHT MASS, SOLEMNITY OF THE NATIVITY OF THE LORD, Vatican
Basilica, Wednesday, 24 December 2014

Those Long-Standing Traditions
FIRST VESPERS ON THE SOLEMNITY OF MARY, MOTHER OF GOD AND TE
DEUM IN THANKSGIVING FOR THE PAST YEAR, Vatican Basilica, Saturday, 31
December 2016

Let There Be Light
ADDRESS OF HIS HOLINESS POPE FRANCIS ON THE OCCASION OF THE
LIGHTING OF THE CHRISTMAS TREE IN GUBBIO, Sunday, 7 December 2014

The Empty Chair
MIDNIGHT MASS SOLEMNITY OF THE NATIVITY OF THE LORD, Vatican
Basilica, Saturday, 24 December 2016

Light in the Darkness
MIDNIGHT MASS, SOLEMNITY OF THE NATIVITY OF THE LORD, Vatican
Basilica, Wednesday, 24 December 2014

The Power of Love
"URBI ET ORBI" MESSAGE OF HIS HOLINESS POPE FRANCIS, CHRISTMAS
2016, Central Loggia of the Vatican Basilica, Sunday, 25 December 2016

Seeing with the Eyes of God
MEETING WITH THE PERSONNEL OF THE HOLY SEE AND OF THE VATICAN
CITY STATE WITH THEIR FAMILIES, Paul VI Audience Hall, Thursday, 22
December 2016

The Whole World Being at Peace
MIDNIGHT MASS SOLEMNITY OF THE NATIVITY OF THE LORD, Vatican
Basilica, Saturday, 24 December 2016

The Wonder of an Infant
"URBI ET ORBI" MESSAGE OF HIS HOLINESS POPE FRANCIS, CHRISTMAS
2015, Friday, 25 December 2015

A Time for Family
MEETING WITH THE PERSONNEL OF THE HOLY SEE AND OF THE VATICAN
CITY STATE WITH THEIR FAMILIES, Paul VI Audience Hall, Monday, 21 December
2015

When Our Families Don't Seem So Holy
MIDNIGHT MASS, SOLEMNITY OF THE NATIVITY OF THE LORD, Vatican
Basilica, Wednesday, 24 December 2014

Mary, Mother of God
HOMILY OF HIS HOLINESS POPE FRANCIS ON THE SOLEMNITY OF MARY,
THE HOLY MOTHER OF GOD, WORLD DAY OF PEACE, Vatican Basilica,
Sunday, 1 January 2017

As the Year Draws to a Close
FIRST VESPERS ON THE SOLEMNITY OF MARY, MOTHER OF GOD AND TE DEUM IN THANKSGIVING FOR THE PAST YEAR, Vatican Basilica, Saturday, 31 December 2016

A Flight into Egypt
ADDRESS OF HIS HOLINESS POPE FRANCIS TO THE DONORS OF THE CRIB AND THE CHRISTMAS TREE IN ST. PETER'S SQUARE, Paul VI Audience Hall, Friday, 9 December 2016

Follow the Star
HOLY MASS ON THE SOLEMNITY OF THE EPIPHANY OF THE LORD, Vatican Basilica, Friday, 6 January 2017

Arise, Shine, Go Forth
EUCHARISTIC CELEBRATION ON THE SOLEMNITY OF THE EPIPHANY OF THE LORD, Vatican Basilica, Wednesday, 6 January 2016

Our Life Is a Journey
EUCHARISTIC CELEBRATION ON THE SOLEMNITY OF THE EPIPHANY OF THE LORD, Vatican Basilica, Monday, 6 January 2014

Returning to Nazareth
HOMILY OF HIS HOLINESS POPE FRANCIS, Vatican Basilica, Sunday, 27 December 2015

About the Author

Diane M. Houdek is the author of *The Joy of Advent, Pope Francis and Our Call to Joy, Lent with St. Francis,* and *Advent with St. Francis.* She is a professed Secular Franciscan with a bachelor's degree in English and history from Marquette University and a master's degree in English literature from Northwestern University. She is the digital book editor for Franciscan Media and past editor of *Weekday Homily Helps* and *Bringing Home the Word.*